TREES

by Rebecca Phillips-Bartlett

Minneapolis, Minnesota

Credits

All images are courtesy of Shutterstock.com, unless otherwise specified. With thanks to Getty Images, Thinkstock Photo, and iStockphoto. Recurring – elyomys, nblx. Cover – Guliveris. 4–5 – A3pfamily, by-studio. 6–7 – tiverylucky, vlad09, mjurik, Triff. 8–9 – siambizkit, Nadezhda Aniukhina, ElenaPhotos. 10–11 – basel101658, Lightspring, rsooll, Tatyana Mi. 12–13 – leungchopan, zlikovec, billysfam. 14–15 – Smileus, Alexander Tolstykh. 16–17 – JP Chret, Koverninska Olga, happiness69. 18–19 – Anne Coatesy, Massimiliano Paolino. 20–21 – 3523studio, Dariush M, borchee, jdross75. 22–23 – seamind224, Mama Belle and the kids.

Bearport Publishing Company Product Development Team

President: Jen Jenson; Director of Product Development: Spencer Brinker; Managing Editor: Allison Juda; Associate Editor: Naomi Reich; Associate Editor: Tiana Tran; Art Director: Colin O'Dea; Designer: Kim Jones; Designer: Kayla Eggert; Product Development Assistant: Owen Hamlin

Library of Congress Cataloging-in-Publication Data is available at www.loc.gov or upon request from the publisher.

ISBN: 979-8-88916-953-6 (hardcover)
ISBN: 979-8-88916-957-4 (paperback)
ISBN: 979-8-89232-130-3 (ebook)

© 2025 BookLife Publishing
This edition is published by arrangement with BookLife Publishing.

North American adaptations © 2025 Bearport Publishing Company. All rights reserved. No part of this publication may be reproduced in whole or in part, stored in any retrieval system, or transmitted in any form or by any means, electronic, mechanical, photocopying, recording, or otherwise, without written permission from the publisher. Bearport Publishing is a division of Chrysalis Education Group.

For more information, write to Bearport Publishing, 5357 Penn Avenue South, Minneapolis, MN 55419.

CONTENTS

Plenty of Plants 4
Terrific Trees 5
Tree Features 6
Losing Their Leaves 10
Green for Good 12
Tree Needs 14
Food from Trees 16
Home Sweet Home 18
Identifying Trees 20
Talking about Trees 22
Glossary 24
Index 24

PLENTY OF PLANTS

Our world is full of amazing plants. They grow in many shapes, sizes, and colors.

Let's explore this *plant-iful* world all around us!

PLANTS CAN GROW IN THE GROUND, IN WATER, OR ON OTHER THINGS.

TERRIFIC TREES

There are more than 60,000 types of trees on Earth. They help keep our planet healthy. Some trees can live for hundreds or even thousands of years.

TREE FEATURES

TRUNKS

Trees can look very different from one another. However, there are some things that they all have in common.

Trees have wooden stems called trunks that hold them up. Most of the time, trunks get thicker and stronger as trees grow.

TREE TRUNKS GROW NEW WOOD IN LAYERS CALLED RINGS.

Growth rings inside a trunk

BARK

Trunks are covered in bark. This helps **protect** trees from things that can harm them, such as bad weather and **insects**. Trees have different kinds of bark.

OAK TREES HAVE BROWN, BUMPY BARK.

BIRCH TREES HAVE SMOOTH, WHITE BARK.

WHAT KIND OF BARK DO TREES NEAR YOU HAVE?

ROOTS

All trees have roots. Most roots grow under the ground. The web of growth helps keep trees from falling over. Roots also take in water and **nutrients** from the soil.

Roots

SOMETIMES, TREE ROOTS GROW ON TOP OF THE GROUND.

BRANCHES AND LEAVES

Long branches grow out from the trunk near the top part of a tree. Leaves grow on smaller sticks from these branches.

Leaves

Branch

YOU CAN SOMETIMES TELL THE KIND OF TREE FROM THE SHAPE OF ITS LEAVES.

LOSING THEIR LEAVES

Have you ever noticed that some trees look different when the **seasons** change? Their leaves are green during the summer but change color and drop to the ground in the fall. Trees that lose their leaves are called **deciduous** (di-SIJ-oo-uhs).

LEAVES MAY TURN RED, YELLOW, ORANGE, OR BROWN IN THE FALL.

Why do deciduous trees do this? They have thin leaves that would freeze and die in the winter. This would hurt the trees. Losing their leaves helps deciduous trees stay healthy.

GREEN FOR GOOD

Some trees have green leaves all year. These are called **evergreen** trees. Their leaves are slowly growing all the time.

Needles

Scales

Many evergreen tree leaves are very different from those of other plants. These leaves are small but thick. They are often called needles or scales. The leaves have a waxy covering that protects them from the cold.

THE WAXY COVERING ALSO HELPS EVERGREEN LEAVES KEEP IN WATER.

TREE NEEDS

Plants make their own food. Trees use water, nutrients, sunlight, and **carbon dioxide** to make the sugary food they need to grow.

FOOD FROM TREES

People get some kinds of food from trees. Many fruits and nuts, such as apples and hazelnuts, grow on trees.

SOME TREES ARE **POISONOUS**. ALWAYS ASK A GROWN-UP BEFORE PICKING PLANTS.

Many animals count on trees for food, too. Some eat the fruits and nuts that trees grow. Other animals munch on the leaves and bark.

SQUIRRELS AND PORCUPINES EAT BARK.

GIRAFFES AND ELEPHANTS EAT LEAVES.

HOME SWEET HOME

Many animals make their homes in trees. Some birds use leaves and twigs to build nests in the branches. Other birds peck holes in the trunks and live inside the tree.

Many insects live underneath a tree's bark or on its leaves. Some animals use parts of trees for **shelter**. Hedgehogs often **hibernate** for the winter in piles of fallen leaves.

IDENTIFYING TREES

There are many different types of trees. Can you match the descriptions below to the pictures on page 21?

1. Pine trees have needle-shaped leaves that stay green all year.

2. Aspen trees have smooth, white bark. Their leaves are green in the summer and turn yellow in the fall.

3. Oak trees have bumpy, brown bark and leaves with curved edges. They grow nuts called acorns.

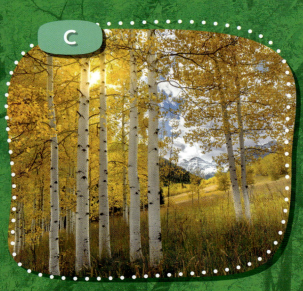

Answers: 1) Pine trees are A. 2) Aspen trees are C. 3) Oak trees are B.

21

TALKING ABOUT TREES

Different kinds of trees grow all around the world. Think about the trees where you live. Do they look the same all year, or do they change with the seasons?

Next time you go outside, look at the trees near you. What does their bark look like? What are the shapes and colors of their leaves? Write down what you see. There are plenty of plants to explore!

GLOSSARY

carbon dioxide a gas in the air that plants need to survive

deciduous having leaves that fall off every year

evergreen having green leaves all year

hibernate to go into a sleeplike state during periods of cold weather

insects small animals that have six legs and three main body parts

nutrients natural substances that plants and animals need to grow and stay healthy

poisonous able to harm or kill if eaten

protect to keep safe from harm

seasons parts of the year with different weather

shelter a safe place that covers and protects animals

INDEX

animals 17–19
bark 7, 17, 19–20, 23
food 14, 16–17
fruit 16–17
leaves 9–13, 15, 17–20, 23
roots 8, 15
seasons 10, 22
sunlight 14–15
trunks 6–7, 9, 15, 18
water 4, 8, 13–15